Jacob:

I think you also seem like a super
solid dude. I can't wait to
share poems!

YESYES BOOKS

Best,
[signature]

D1600462

PORTLAND, OREGON

MAN vs. SKY

POEMS

COREY ZELLER

First Edition, 2013
978-1-936919-13-0
Printed in the United States of America.

Published by YesYes Books
1232 NE Prescott Street
Portland, OR 97211

YesYesBooks.com

YESYES BOOKS
KMA Sullivan, Publisher
Justin Boening, Senior Editor
Stephen Danos, Assistant Editor
Hafizah Geter, Assistant Editor
Jill Kolongowski, Assistant Editor
Thomas Patrick Levy, Website Design and Development
Mark Derks, Fiction Editor, *Vinyl Poetry*
Phillip B. Williams, Poetry Editor, *Vinyl Poetry*

For Jeremy Quezada

Man vs. Sky is a collection of prose poems written in the voice of the author's close friend following his suicide on January 13th, 2012.

Contents

31	I made constellations with a pencil I poked holes in the boxes
32	The clear fields in a dying horse's eye
33	There is a kingdom in the wind with no king
34	The sighs I must one day give to my skull
35	He began as a mark in the dust not a word
36	Cross your fingers
37	While I am dreaming of submarines
38	And the fire was like a chandelier
39	Before men could speak they enjoyed confounding one another with signs
40	Figured out what the evening sun did at night
41	The left side of my body was a cloud
42	When they discovered the wheel they done the wrong thing with it
43	The clock on the bed and the white horse sad as the island
44	And all these old ugly white women saying
45	Nailed up the Chinaberry
46	Night was nothing to him but a song
47	She was water I cupped my hands
48	Tonight the gars on the trees are swords in the hands of knights
49	My teacher has a tongue like a cow
50	We burned the headdress in the fog
51	Because none of you know what you want follow me
52	I lose in infinity those blades of grass that cut you in the dark
53	It was shedding its skin like a God sheds his grace

I am going to do a few things can't nobody follow

I am going to be a sputtering gray zeppelin in what used to be sky, the wah-wah pedal wind and everything else. I am going to show you up with congas and weird smiles, a touch without skin, skin for eyes. If you perceive a lake before you then you perceive me, my body, a wide low place of drowning. *Watch*: I am going to do one thing that will leave you breathless. I am going to make you perform a great act of sorrow, over and over, after me. *Watch, repeat.* Look at you all: tumbling down, hanging there. You didn't know you were loose rocks shaken out of a mountain after eons and eons of waiting and try, after my seismic went. You can feel it now though, this tough, invisible tie to the air. You've always been floating. Just pick up your feet and watch.

When the rest of you were busy being children

I made a man out of bicycle parts, a stereo inside the air, basement reverberations. I was mud and cargo shorts, the long grass behind the cul-de-sac where kids hid warm beer, oily rainbows in your backyard pools, endless bare feet. I can't hide from you anymore. You are a part of my open head, chasms of stoned things, lots and lots of useless staring. You should see it here, be here. The trees sizzle like long stems of broccoli inside a black pan. The glass leaps into the ground and vice versa. Everything blurs but you.

I'll just bleed so the stars can have something dark to shine in

A coughing space, room to stretch down and touch their pointed toes. Imagine: the stars dancing around like cartoons, perfect and faceless. Imagine: I'll never see a single one again. I can't tell you what color the floors are here, if there are streetlights outside, who is walking through the hallways. I can't tell you anything anymore. The world drifts from me the way ice drifts from the space where the water breaks through. It dissolves on its own, year after year, stitches sown out of the cold.

The piano under the water looks like a shark

Bare and white as lightning, as your plainest song. The thud you feel walking, talking, is a wire missing to a piano key. I pound it with my finger, hear a note no one else believes in, one only those without throats can sing. I pound it feeling my chest open. My chest a bathtub filled with toucans, uncontrollable jets of green-blue blood. This is to say: the piano under the water looks like a piano but is really a casket. The lid of it opens and pours me out. If I could, I'd push my teeth back into my head like piano keys but I can't push or pull anything now. The flat of my hands hold the water and the water holds me still. I mistake the sea things for street things, jellyfish for lightning, bobbing and blinking as they do, deeper into the dark. It is then I realize: this is not a casket, this is not a piano, and you are not the sea.

Blazing a trail in black water

I rise, not moving. There is no width to these spaces now. Everything is an opening. Everything careens. There is no such thing as heart or tongue. If I make a simple step here it becomes a small cage, rolling back into other cages, a large misshapen body of slots and bars. There is nothing to put inside it or me. Instead, I wait here, where the branches above the water are black shawls, all pointing the same way, threadbare and deliberate. There are no angels to speak of here. If there are any, anywhere, they are not winged people, raging stallions. They are simply pieces of different animals, collected, suspended in midair, galloping into a distance that never really was a distance, galloping until there is nothing left of them but the sound of birds being born underwater, the sound of the wind dreaming of stillness, the stillness dreaming of me.

I dream the sick roses sitting up in their blood at your feet

Growing like the sun, the real sun, pulling itself out of the rusted belly of the earth. Inside the sun, millions of broken antlers shovel through burning rocks as another blank day rides the back of an orange month. No calendar can touch it or me. I dream the sounds the sun makes are really my little brother tearing apart our house with his little teeth. Below it, he finds the skeleton of an infant. Now you know where I've been.

I see your dress sleeping in the closet

I sleep inside it too, with whatever kind of air is left of me. Black matter is my new job. There's nothing more to say about it outside of all these glasses and jackets and shoes I've found that were once, probably, worn by someone somewhere, maybe you. I stand in the street and hear many voices that are not mine. I believe, though, in these tiny strips of, these notations on such and such. In an apartment, in Chinatown, a person who is not me tinkers with a handle that is not in the wall, thinking the wall is a music box, thinking there is a handle. A small song tries to make a sound but doesn't, can't. The neighbors shout and call the cops for all the noise not there.

And then I noticed there were no young men

No old ones either. There was no low breathing, no disturbed fuses and flophouse laughter, nothing to be said about crack pipes or tatter or fractions. Just trees: what Dante says happens to us in a certain circle. These crooked things living on their own voices, their same sounds. Bark peels from them without the wind having to help. They are terrified of themselves and their tallness. Don't get it twisted, Dante baby. They do not cry out for having had a piece of them broken, for having bled again. They cry only because their branches sometimes reach each other out of the long dry stillness. They cry out, quivering, simply for having touched.

Like a hot bath in the light in the west

I am feeding something that doesn't want to be. If you could hear it, you'd say it had a voice like a doll's blue dress, white sleeves. You'd say: *it is the tiniest thing I'll never touch* and you'd mean it, somehow, even as you carried it with you, to me. Ask me what happened to my lips. Ask me why they are so closed, so different and burned. Ask. I will tell you how kissing up her leg was like unwrapping the same gift over and over. A gift until I realized what it was. How it had left, alive. How it leaves me, still.

A dream like a plaid shirt that takes forever to fall to the floor

Is still just a dream. My chest cavity is a window of plaid. I unbutton it. I am standing in the room I died in. The wall here is made of plaid, the body in the bed too. What pushes inside me is not a heart. It is a hummingbird with tartan wings, a beak as thin and sore as a child's broken arm. It is whatever you cannot imagine the air can do, a choice between all the air in the world and none at all.

I the rider

Without shaking, her hips, newly without, ash where a fire never was, burned. I: the last part of the earth that meets the sky, dizzied. I: patron saint of public restroom walls and exploding white masks, pegs and nude paintings, the swells of a guitar pick streaming gang signs and broken Coke bottles. I: the circulatory system of subways slept in, our clumsy stealing. I: a set-list, a scrap of notebook paper blown into the world, into and into, the way I tumbled into her clean mouth and couldn't find my way back out, back to where I held her, still, unraveling in my arms like a therapy session, a depression like teething, cop voices. She swallows hard and I am almost there. It is almost like kissing.

I know some by signs others by whispers

A body like a package that says *tear here*, a mouth that comes apart. Whatever is left inside is identical like pills or cotton swabs. Whatever is left inside is crumbs and battering, a soft thing you said, as if on paper, random letters inside it erased. Yes, I'm drunk. Inside my bottle you hear hummingbirds but it is filled with nothing but Thursday upon Thursday, the blue hair of a stranger, your mother's birthday. Inside the bottle she holds herself in her hands, what you mistake as little candles. *Happy birthday*, she says. She sings it to herself.

I swear to you more children will be born

From the crawl spaces, pieces of your first house. The world is big enough for them to look like me, bleached knobs for eyes, knots in their faces. Their absence will be like glue when they find the forest, gone phonetically; no one will worry about them. When someone dreams of them, they will dream of an old man who skins rabbits on the porch of his house. The rabbits are in the grass: skinned but moving, making the grass as pink as their veins. The sounds they make are that of a guitar when it is all alone. It leans against a wall, choking.

He said please master I am so ugly I see myself in the floor

This is part of a memory I am having. I couldn't hear him over the sound of the microwave. Inside it: little things hummed in an orange tree, melting down to nothing, a heartthrob. The people in the room, in the memory, revolve on a transparent disk. The table before them is deflating. They'd be looking at me, in the corner, if they had faces left, eyes. What a person is has nothing to do with what they are. They are coating over a shell, spaces where they used to go.

I have insomnia over apples

Nothing was there to watch me. The skin peeled off easier than
you'd imagine. Hour by hour, the smell of them opened the
room, unused white circles of meat. Something told me not to.
Something told me that I was studying a rupture, what only just
touches the air but stays like notes on liner sheets. Hung. The
windows were fogged. Hands rubbed pictures into them, a life
over a life, no steam. She was soaking in the bath. Clear images
formed on the water, only half of her was there. I let my hand
fall in. I was as much an animal as a god could be, a maelstrom of
wasps, handfuls of the wrong face.

He is in his second mind, my mind

A fallout shelter, one dingy basement below the other, a place to stave off, be sorry. I shuffle through my memory which is monotone, yellow pages. Every business listed is a company specializing in cementing windows, unfixing doors, collecting zeroes. You call and the number is busy. You call and hear yourself breathing on the other end. Whatever I did to deserve this is like the clouds: crisp with misinformation, leashing. I sit fixing something which turns out to be a human bone. It bends now, on its own. I adjust my head with my hands, up where a light should be. It is not a light but a keyhole a man is watching me through. I look at the door, waiting for the knob to turn. I look into the keyhole: another empty room.

I know the girl feeling the kiss in the mirror

So I can sleep in peace I build a small house inside a large one. It expands, deflates, expands. It is breathing. Inside it: a perfect copy of our old living room. I pretend we are talking about bad movies, band posters. I pretend you are saying something about the empty clotheslines between my teeth, my cassette face, a cork that keeps the world from going in. I move the chairs around the way I think you'd ask me to. I fit so well inside my body now that it's not there.

Because I'm not going anywhere

Because the grease spots wouldn't come off my clothes, like rosacea, a knot in a bike chain, ink blots in a guidance counselor's office you said looked like giants eating mopeds, a burning well, half-made birdhouses, bit nails. Because I am tired of their memories of me, their amusement parks of grief, their tilt-a-whirl crying. Because I lied when I said I'd call, another *otherwise*, a country of injury, specifics. Because I owned something like a résumé, wrote a résumé, altered it. Because there is artwork in airports, glowing walls beside what seems like endless escalators, drooping underground. Because I deleted all my music, my oxygen, my Chilean, my eyes the empty shells of avocados, color strips on a burnt-out screen. Because I heard, almost always, a dial tone where a voice should be, a constant chord. Because of you, I'm gone.

Wolf milk there was a mother wolf standing in the tub

She had the beautiful breasts of a woman, sharp nipples, but was howling, the tub screeching against the movement of her skin. The sky outside was the color of lamb. No one had known how sick they were until they could read the letters painted on the sides of buildings. No one knew until they were taught. A screen door was hanging like a baby tooth from our gum-colored house and my baby brother was crying out where I could not see him. School never lets out here. Kids with animal heads sit in class. Their teacher is only strips of ribs and meat hung on strings about the room, the sound of what falls from them. Their only lesson is to sit and wait for what will not come, the blackness that pushes the room into its one, bare bulb, the sound of it, swinging.

You splendid animal circling the gables of the blind

Someone is praying a terrible prayer. They do not know what holds them on their knees is their body, their bending, one rung among so many missing. Your fingers push icons back and forth on a computer screen, reflecting you, what you might call *reflecting*, a life led on little squares of light. The sea swallows inside the sound of the bird; the sound of the bird becomes the sea, a digital one, static that goes on and on. Your child, too, cannot sleep. He stands at the window, as night becomes morning, trying to click and drag something he sees in the air across the sky.

Of the red liquid in my fingers where I have lain out naked

I have nothing to say. Paul Celan has become a fountain. He pours blonde birds from his mouth that peck each other to death. If not that, they build their own cages to soon peck each other to death. Neruda is the same as he was before. He reaches inside his fat stomach and pulls out flowers to pass to the skeletons of women. He says: *if you still had hair I would wind myself in it like a tarantula, wind it round my neck till it was the only thing that held me between the air and the light.* The skeletons stick the stems through their ribs. The flowers in their bellies make them look like cherry blossom trees, petals floating from them as they walk away.

Look at my legs I am the Nijinsky of dreams

Gravity harms us. Were it not for us, our bodies, we'd be beautiful, dancers. We'd be stop-motioned, radiant, woven together like French braids. My legs are still dangling. I am trying to pull the whole world up by my chin. My mouth opens and my eyes close as if I am about to sing.

I made constellations with a pencil I poked holes in the boxes

But couldn't get out. I am part of a new world of cardboard. I stare out the punctures. What I see beyond them is not a smooth white, not abrasions and monikers, but a history of rooms. People float above the floor through spaces where they used to live, are no longer. What am I now that no one calls my name, now that I'm not cheekbones and hair and fingers over a guitar? I don't know. Lines of light shoot through the box like trip wires in a spy movie. I write our names on the wall, pluses between us. I write you reasons to live, reasons you can't read in the dark.

The clear fields in a dying horse's eye

Blue sky, cloud after cloud passing through a black iris. What else is there to know but that everything ends? You go to a place where there are no people, no houses, no windows. There is nothing to look in or out of, nothing to harbor or hide. Alone: you simply move through yourself, haunted, a lonely banter. Ask me: what is there to tell the air if it doesn't even believe in itself, when it has yet to find an equal? In the open space, your body might as well be a ceiling, a ceremony of inches and hair, fingerprints like doors. You're a surface that the world is washing clean, over and over, till it can see its own face inside you. What it sees is a whole history of bodies made of hands. What it sees it calls a ghost.

There is a kingdom in the wind with no king

If I hover it is from a cage which hangs from a chain, a maroon kite caught in the exhausted sky. The wings here are microscopic, blank spaces in an unfinished game of hangman, frozen light. Everything is unnamed, most of all me. My hands pass through the walls without me trying, rudders sailing through floral pattern, ripples of paint and plaster. I am held here, in this old life, like a cube of ice in a clear glass of water. The birds look up at me and not the other way around.

The sighs I must one day give to my skull

Will come like colorless flowers, cheat codes, my young body buried below birds. The streets have learned to eat themselves to stay alive. There's nowhere to walk now. Everything is a letter I might have written you, scrawled in chicken scratch across the horizon. Or maybe a car that only vaguely looks like yours, passing by me on my way to work, no one inside it.

He began as a mark in the dust not a word

A squabbling of dusk and squares. No one knew anything but the tidiness of the antennas, the slow plow of day in and day out, averages. I am covered in plastic. It breathes through me like a vacuum, keyboard cleaner in a teenager's mouth. Red drips from the ceiling, sparkling like mica, making the room glow a bright tangerine. You and I are caught in some kind of prism. We are polymer. You pull my hand to your chest. I know what you want me to feel but I won't.

Cross your fingers

And fall into the spaces. Your lowest sounds fill the pipes, make them tremble, turn the water a kind of sea color you can't get rid of, can't get used to drinking. I am about the size of a cocktail umbrella now. I am feeling a bit woozy. I look at the sky and name it after you. I name it after you because it is eating itself. Pieces of it are falling everywhere, jutting out of the ground like glass. Everywhere you walk is a kind of pre-hurt, a fear of getting cut. Everywhere you walk you have to shield your eyes from the shine.

While I am dreaming of submarines

Clouds pour out like suits. The suits hold you, your starched bodies, what you call naked. You will never unwrap. Everywhere is sad because it doesn't last but still goes on, filling, an accidental all. I pass you through the pressure weather, a fish battering itself against the rocks, silver sides that flash and flash and flash. I am a periscope that only sees into itself. If you run your finger along the surface of where I just was you'll find gills in the air and along the walls. Nothing has to breathe on its own.

And the fire was like a chandelier

A grenade of soft, wet diamonds. In the complete black, a small door opened and your face appeared. You were laughing at me through a square of light, a resurrection of proteins and healthy tans. You were laughing at me and your laughter was a city of cut green paper. Your laughter was snub-faced and back alley, blinking like ancient neon, a noir of sound. You are no longer there in the frame. A light blinks at the end of the dark, another door left open. I have forever to watch it go out.

Before men could speak they enjoyed confounding one another with signs

Smoke is coming through the bottom of the door even though your hands are already burned. They windmill the air now: a slight composite, analog, white against black. I feel it. The black in the white is feeding it. The paper makes a shape like a mouth. A body opens one of its circles. Things turn as half things, opposite of themselves, paper ships inside an oven. The family is getting ready for dinner. One frame marks out the next, the smaller of which is always the larger, a victor of spoils. The picture is already gone.

Figured out what the evening sun did at night

It bathes itself in silver, makes up new names for morning, like someone else's clothes in moving boxes, like everything that splits simply to meet again. Touch the air and call it skin, my skin, yours. Pretend. You will triumph where others failed. You will be apparent, your life split-screened with a better one, examined, pointed-out, made an example of. Nod. If you are thirsty, accept anything else but exactly what you want to drink. We share the cup. This is living. Drink.

The left side of my body was a cloud

Mess, you cannot move it. You pause. You wonder what to do with the music strapping you down. Who will teach you to blur now, if not this, this diatonic scale? In a room, a table blinks on and off. There is a crackling sound like burning in our shared closet. I feed cracks under the doors, music notes I draw with a pencil on ripped scraps of paper: *B-Minor*, *A-Flat*, *D-Sharp*, *accidentals*. These are the types of things you do at the end of the world. The air dislocates like a shoulder from this part of the house simply because I stand inside it. It feels me and spasms in frequency, arbitrarily, an accumulation. I download. I hold a shirt she left behind like an answer I didn't want to get.

When they discovered the wheel they done the wrong thing with it

It is always that way with invention, these diagrams and charts, machines that look like the insides of hummingbirds. Sentences dye themselves colors we haven't seen and dry themselves, on the rocks, in the sun, on their own. They look tacky, a kind of flea market of syntax and emphasis, undignified patterns, punctuation like early flying machines, the kind you pedal in. They are not a part of us. This is the long way of saying I never liked talking. I am searching for something else people can do inside these bleached headphones. I am bobbing my head to static. I cite myself in the white.

The clock on the bed and the white horse sad as the island

Neither can tell me what time it is because time is a mirror made wrong. I am the one behind the rounded glass. I am the long hand and short, moving my arms and legs over numbers and lines. Each one cuts a little. Each one a sharp rivet over what I'm losing. Comply. The TV is an empty shell. The mirror is easier. You just have to find a frame to stand in, to hold still. *What time is it?* I am late for something. There are still things left I was supposed to do, appointments no one crossed off. Are you lonely? It is May. I am not so happy about it. Instead, I think of the name of the woman who drove to die so long I forget it. I think of other names too. How *Heather*, for instance, is not just a name. I think of homophones. Finally, I have become what I always wanted: a room without a door, a field without sky.

And all these old ugly white women saying

Acceptance, their heads turning like ceiling fans turned all the way up in halfway houses, their concerns dotting the beige sky, something without teeth, how people here talk about Jesus, an alabaster one, abs of steel on TV, arms opening on the mountain. *Talk about your savior*, they say, *accept*. You are petty and small. You are the ghost of a blood-colored bird. You are the way the clouds stay close to the mountain. So close, you cannot tell which rolls out of which. *Don't be afraid*, they say. You hum your own dissolve.

Nailed up the Chinaberry

You were not shared. The land was gone as well and what piled in its place made things disappear, wither, and contract like a snake opening up to fit a lamb inside it. A beautiful, pink sound came and went. The child became drops of something almost liquid. I was videotape around you, a videocassette of a child's birthday party, people waving at the camera. It was the eighties. The lighting in the room was bad. The kid was wearing a Transformers shirt. The family was a family but could morph into something else, something darker and powerful, machinery. I cannot make out their faces but I know they've been smiling too long, uncomfortably long. I wish I could you tell you how bad this hurts.

Night was nothing to him but a song

We were stopped on a road. Everything was a hot air balloon tied to the grass, bouncing up and down. We were afraid it would all simply go, begin going into the gone light. We were afraid of worse things too. I kept asking everyone if I was clear, if they could see me. I was surprised I didn't have to try. We were playing that game where everything was lava only we never stopped. Look at all the things we could have touched.

She was water I cupped my hands

Stratocumulus bodies, how we pointed at people in the mall and guessed what they looked like among the sky of store signs: *that one's a pony, that one's a revolver, that one's a person, a carton of milk, a raincoat.* We were lying on the linoleum floor in the food court. We had pictures of each other in our pockets, our faces and hands scratched out with a quarter, cumulus heads. We had nothing of ourselves, of us. Everything was going to be fine.

Tonight the gars on the trees are swords in the hands of knights

Their armor is made of a red bark like bleeding. They are above themselves. Everything stops for the sound of their screeching arms which fall off as they swing, their swords sticking out of the ground like marijuana plants. This is to say that someone needs to be saved somewhere. The feelings about it are too ripe, swelling like fetuses. Right now, a knight is riding an old-fashioned bicycle. Right now, a knight is riding what he thinks is a bicycle but is really a man holding an ace of spades between his teeth. They are part of a war that has lasted twenty-seven years. The object of the war is not to speak.

My teacher has a tongue like a cow

The boys wore red polo shirts and the girls wore plaid skirts, both were annunciations. We were waiting for something. Chalk dust made the air thick enough to weigh, hold. We were waiting for our bones to stretch out of our skin, to be more than tiny skins. I was whispering in the ear of the boy next to me. I was telling him there is a meaning to all the bodies, telling him how to open the glass. He was brown hair and light eyes. He was the soft part of a knife, his face a plastic bag over the moon's damaged head, sucking in and out where a mouth should be. We waited there the way I waited for her later: dutiful, hands crossed, pledging allegiance. When she came back it was like learning your very first secret and watching it snap in half. It was being the light, eating the light, yet staying the blackest thing.

We burned the headdress in the fog

I am playing gin rummy with your mother. I am staring down her pink bathrobe at her tits. On the cards there are pictures of your mother crying and the cards are crying on the table which has no legs. They are wet and crying and she is crying too because you are fourteen and behind a dumpster with other fourteen year olds getting high because being fourteen is hard. Because being fourteen is an abandoned building of *sorry*, mine shafts of *care*, is one touch too soon. Because being fourteen is a tatter of open eyes, one whole year of dirty hair, mesh and voicemails and condensed music that has nothing to do with the awkward way you talk. Because being fourteen is like being a billboard in a forest of sinking trees that advertises trees and blinks a tree time at every hour. Only the trees know what it means and whatever it means is sad like staring down your mother's bathrobe. She wins every hand. Nothing has changed.

Because none of you know what you want follow me

You will be here too, a slab on a clean surface, a final nakedness. Days will exist without your help, squinting at their existing, at fell things, an overture of figures. New men will admire newer ones. They will shout at television sets or something like television sets. Downtowns will change. Main Streets will be crushed into the numb heat and silence of their own dead paint. What is left of us will shine a quiet fading, will shudder like a girl with fingers between her, an awkward hand up a blouse, spring and cleavage, a moaning of chandeliers. Even now, your life bites your death's lip, parts its sleeping hair. You've grown apt at this waking, this opening and closing of doors. You will pass and pass. You will learn another way. You will speak the language of old photographs, of dirt and stone, the gray teeth jutting out of the ground. You will speak this burning across the sky. Let it hold you down.

I lose in infinity those blades of grass that cut you in the dark

Those hours of weary chiming, legs over legs, hair against not, an ordinary story, what flew nowhere in the blue lines of maps. The animals beyond us learn love and so they kill each other. What is there to do? The dark is so full of cutting, of sharpness, birds folding. It is full of the laughter that pulls in and warns itself. It is full, yet asks for more. It opens its mouth to be fed. There is never enough to throw.

It was shedding its skin like a God sheds his grace

I mistake the adjustment for innocence, the crematory for a player piano. What song is this, lit up? What notes thick themselves over the walls, blue and red and orange through my sleeping chest? I told myself, before being strung-up, that I was the bread of life. But what bread do you know of turns to ash when it is put in the oven? What bread do you know of is placed on a mantel, becoming a part of a room, its adjustments, sinking further into itself like a star? Dust to dust, I strum the silence. It opens again. I cannot believe how much of me was left behind. How it rises out of the unleavened dark.

Like someone throwing guitars at me like bats that come out of a black hole

It is too ripe to touch, your hand goes through. Don't. You are more ligature than has-been, you are tying and tying and pulled apart. You are the fiscal year, pajamas worn to a cloud apocalypse, float and sink. You are the pretext of a prize no one is allowed to win, the graffiti-covered billboards walking on their own down the streets of a ghost town like Jerry Bruckheimer robots, bliss. You are my dead arms shining in the dark, tinkering in a basement. You are bad paintings of Jesus, the sacred heart, a poor rendering of our savior blessing kids on a playground swing. You are whoever would paint that kind of shit. You are guilty because you're alive and I am not. Your guilt is ectoplasm on strangers. You fly into them like that green floating glob in Ghostbusters. Your head is filled with old theme songs. You are used to this kind of attention.

I sleep with my arm around whoever is sleeping

Text messages are falling out of her phone onto the ground. She is laughing like she is about to cry, afflicted with corners and somnambulant animals. She is infected: her same voice every morning, how the light fills the rooms without touching her. We need to stop. This road is filled with so many holes they fall into each other. It is like the moment you forget you're pouring a glass of milk and it spills over. Only it is her, happening, so much of her, pouring out. I have never seen her this way. She is so full.

Death who also says forget the lost child throwing photographs at the moon

I am building the color red. It is easy because it is my death. There are pieces of it everywhere like debris on the shore. I don't know where it comes from but each piece fits perfectly where I put it. It is like a jigsaw puzzle without the hassle, without the time. It is like making the scene of a shipwreck out of burning candles. Everything is candles; everything is burning and red, even the sea.

I think I would respect humming if I couldn't hear it

Get down. The sunlight whizzes past your head like bullets in an army movie. Crawl on your hands and knees. The light wants you back. It looks out of itself, in, and you are its flammable reflection. Don't hesitate. You are bare and shedding and don't reassemble. You are truth at the end of the day's double-barrel, flocks of thrown glass moving, some handed crayon picture of your saddest day. You are instead, bedrooms of angel dust hacking and your fingers that smell like inside her. Still, it wants you back. It doesn't care you're dirty, doesn't care who fucked you and when, what your GPA was in high school, it doesn't. You're a chapter in the gasping, a book of nothing coming. You read the blankness.

I shut my jaw and my dream teeth crack

Your first arm is the broken one. Your second is the one that holds her around her waist, kissing the first of many disappearing parts. The sky outside reminds me of that scene in JAWS where the men are sitting in the cabin of the boat singing sailor songs. What I'm saying is that I am rocking in it. I am filled with it. And you, what are you to do but feel what most certainly lurks beyond you in a day so blue it's dark? It halfway takes you. Look down. I am sure by now your legs are gone.

I know the staircase that leads into the forest

We are watching a film about the trumpet player who loses his mouth. We are part of the blur that comes between frames, the pink static. We are sitting on the stage of a stadium adorned with the furniture from my childhood living room. Balloons are falling everywhere. I am dressed in a blue jumpsuit with white stars around the collar. I am wearing star glasses. I have a star shaved into my beard. When I cough, or sneeze, three or four people clap from far away. On the screen, the trumpet player is cutting the skin where his mouth used to be. What he makes is not a mouth. He puts the trumpet to the space and everything falls inside.

Buzzing like a hornets' nest full of snakeskins made by the sparrow

My friends envy the snow. They will show you how. They will cut the shape of a bear in the lime green future and practically be clean. The bear shape will stalk through the suburbs of the past eating nothing but reefer and trash in back of Taco Bell and blood. Your friends will talk about science. They will tell you the time machine was a bad idea. They will tell you just as you caress your boyhood face. Just as both of you, young and old, hold hands and disappear.

Knees that can't genuflect anymore

I am a pond made of teeth and wise hair. I am a factory where men draw faces on paper plates all day long, black ink for stubble, lots of little black lines. Here is my face. I am eating off of it in a room the size of an airplane hangar. I move a piece of toast and there is my fake eye. I have a piece of bacon and there is my triangle of a nose. The factory itself does nothing but spill red smoke from its yellow eyes. Meaning: the dead have no idea who is feeding them. Yet they keep being fed, over and over. The end of each brings a new kind of starving. The hunger is another factory. It builds itself.

A raft bearing a granddaddy clock was moored to a black willow

The fish were listening to it tick. I replaced the water they live in. I contained them. I felt them talking. They were wondering how people made love. They decided that it begins with two people nailing white feathers against a gray wall. They decided it ends with them crushing shells on all fours with their bare hands, bare knees. They believe the clocks have something to do with our eyes. They think our eyes are beautiful.

Like two friends of mine who visit me often while I am looking at clouds

You both are standing there, blank as needles. My body is like a bush you've accidentally dropped your keys inside. You are looking through me. You are wet eyed. You know nothing about death but what my shut mouth tells you. The clouds are white fur beyond where you are standing. The clouds are brain-dead animals purring against each other in the blue carpet of sky. You see one stuffed inside my hard remains, my shirt buttoned all the way to the neck. It floats a little out around my neck and makes a sound like a just-born deer. It begins shrieking until an old funeral director comes along and stuffs it back inside. He walks away, shaking what's left of the cloud from what appears to be his hand. It is only then you realize what you've been doing. My corpse has been floating. And you, my friends, have been standing above it only to hold it down.

That smell like water flowers

It is everywhere. It is in the closet that is open, in the CGI walrus on the TV screen talking to kids about algebra, in the money I cannot use. It reminds me that all my best friends have left town forever. It reminds me they cannot call me collect and that calling collect is an ancient form of love. I used to sleep in payphone booths when I was a kid and now they are dinosaurs roaming around junkyards. They are licking the ghosts of cars. They are feeding on kitchen sinks. They are all part of someone's life that no longer is, one they cannot return to, be in, walk around inside. The payphone I used to call you on by the Chinese restaurant was taken out last year. I stand in its absence.

I was worrying about me splitting up the middle

My eyes are two brown seas. Each one is identical to the other in length and depth and brownness. Each one tries to climb into the other over the cliff of my nose. Which is to say: *I cannot stop them from spilling*. Which is to say: *I only go places to drown them*. Today, for instance, I walked into a room and everyone inside it died. I watched them float for hours. Underwater, their heads were like fireworks exploding out of their normal-sized bodies. Hot flashes of color cut the dark water. They did not seem sad to leave. I am happy they're gone.

Death has a knife of sweat and a scabbard of tears

I want you to know I am only crying so I can turn my tears into a lung. I will hang it over chain-link on ghetto bridges. I will hold it to my ghost ear like a boom box when I walk through Oakland. The lung will puff air into nothing, useless as a toy dog. When I take it to your house, you'll pour it tea and ask it how it feels. It will wheeze air. It will slink in and out like a cartoon accordion. You will smile at it the way you smiled at me. You'll say: *don't worry lung, everything will be ok.* You will not care it is made of tears.

I weaved back and forth like a hawk with severed wings

We are standing in front of a cardboard background. It doesn't matter what the background is, whether it is of buildings or the sea. It doesn't matter because we are eating away the image that matters the most. This could mean us, our figures, our nonchalant posing, but it doesn't. We are a daydream a newspaper is having, wet lambs glowing inside a dead TV, initials carved in the Maplewood sky. The fire escapes talk in tongues all around us. They sound like rabbis, witch doctors, a gypsy pounding on the belly of a string-less guitar. The shadows of the leaves look like minnows bonded to the branches. They are trying hard to break away. We know there's no way out.

In the shadows of the charred table I danced once to the pistols

The living you provides discord, a diluted harmony. He spoils, myth-like, forgetting the store-bought paintings that hung in its childhood home. The living you doesn't give a shit about words like postmodern and feels nothing about helplessness. It is nothing but equipment, nothing but you and your mouthful of pills, your ill-fitting sameness. The river beyond the living you, the visible you, is a corpse. I like to watch you swim in its whiteness. It is almost like I am watching you, almost like you are there.

Like strokes of an oar at a river where none have been seen before

I am falling through each floor of the downtown AA center like a ghost's idea of a ghost, sheets and two human holes with eyes inside it. I taste the nothing that lives there, feel it in the needles and blossoms of my chest. I dream of grass stains and lucky hats, Mars colors and disguised offerings, voids and directions. In the room where we just met, I see a man trapped in a bottle like a model ship. He says we are the only ones who can see the bottle. He says we are not falling. He says everything else is falling up.

I know the rich are the only ones that had any good old days

If it is said it is a manipulation, grace in the crosshairs, a life beyond safety. You are present for it and therefore an echo, a disability, a heavy shimmering of danger. Whatever you do, don't touch it, don't hear it. What is uttered will take you. What you utter is what is left of you to take. Sorrows feed like the sparrows and the sparrows feed like the days. The days do their job. They take the world apart.

I am stiff like the amused wilderness

I am held up for people to cry in like a wooden gypsy in a fortunetelling booth. If you put a quarter in the machine a strip of paper will fall out of my mouth. It might say: you are bound to pass between lovers like a spoon. It might say: you've lost something so great it replaced that state of Idaho. It might say: a statue will be made in your honor and erected inside a model train set. A plastic figure in a blue suit will point at it until the man in the fake conductor hat dies. After that, everything will burn as I do in your drained irises. I am jammed in you like a bird in an airplane engine. At the funeral, though, I am the airplane. People step into my casket with their luggage and disappear. I imagine what they are doing in my casket is sitting and waiting, watching a zombie in a stewardess outfit buckle a belt. Her eye is falling out and only one half of her head has hair on it. You though, my friend, are the last person left with my body in the viewing room. You are no longer scared my eyes will open. You hug me and a strip of paper falls out of my mouth. It says: Dear Corey, when you leave the parking lot will be empty. It is snowing.

Acknowledgments

Thank you to the editors of the following journals where these poems first appeared:

Alice Blue Review: "The sighs I must one day give to my skull," "Of the red liquid in my fingers where I have lain out naked"

The AWL: "When they discovered the wheel they done the wrong thing with it"

The Bakery: "I know the staircase that leads into the forest," "I was worrying about me splitting up the middle"

Coconut: "The clear fields in a dying horse's eye," "The clock on the bed and the white horse sad as the island"

The Colorado Review: "I dream the sick roses sitting up in their blood at your feet"

Diode: "I know the girl feeling the kiss in the mirror," "Cross your fingers," "Before men could speak they enjoyed confounding one another with signs," "Night was nothing to him but a song"

ILK: "A dream like a plaid shirt that takes forever to fall to the floor," "He said please master I am so ugly I see myself in the floor," "I weaved back and forth like a hawk with severed wings," "In the shadows of the charred table I danced once to the pistols," "Like strokes of an oar at a river where none have been seen before," "I know the rich are the only ones that had any good old days"

NAP: "She was water I cupped my hands"

OnAndOnScreen: "Like two friends of mine who visit me often while I am looking at clouds"

The Paris-American: "I the rider," "He is in his second mind, my mind"

Sixth Finch: "I shut my jaw and my dream teeth crack"

Smoking Mirrors: "It was shedding its skin like a God sheds his grace"

West Branch: "You splendid animal circling the gables of the blind," "Blazing a trail in black water," "Because none of you know what you want follow me," "Knees that can't genuflect anymore"

I am extremely grateful to KMA Sullivan for believing in this book from the very beginning and for her diligent reading of the poems within. It truly helped me through the grief. Honestly, your love and belief in this work was astonishing.

Thank you to Sean Thomas Dougherty for a decade of friendship, mentoring, brotherhood, concert tickets, cigarettes, edits, and drinks. Huge thanks to Hank Barbour for keeping me alive all these years with conversation and to Jason Arndt for always having my back.

Thanks to Frank Stanford for his words that appear as titles in this book and to C.D. Wright for not being upset when I told her I'd stolen *The Battlefield Where the Moon Says I Love You* at an AWP many years ago when I was broke and hungry for words.

Thank you to George Looney, Tom Noyes, Rick Sadlier, Ralph Reitinger, Elizabeth, Mike, Jason, Zach, Jim and Judy, and to the Quezada family.

Thank you to my grandparents Frank, Marilyn, Colleen, and Harland for their guidance, love, and their great stories of the past.

Thanks to my father Dean Zeller who once sent me 200 dollars in the mail along with a fake acceptance letter from a fake publisher because he felt bad that I was getting rejection letters in the mail every day. I love you.

Thanks to my mother Susan Zeller who, since I was 12, has read hundreds of my poems at her kitchen table. I owe the biggest debt of love and words to you and your faith in me.

Thanks to Michele whose love reminds me every day that there are more important things in life than poems. Thank you for our family and your support. Your love is truly the most important thing to me in this world.

Thanks to Anastasia, for deep companionship. The strength you hold inside you is astounding. I am constantly in awe of you. Thanks to my son Malcolm who was with me as I wrote every poem in this book. I don't live until the moment you open your eyes each day.

Finally, thanks to my friend Jeremy Quezada who believed in my writing long before anyone else did. This book is written in your memory, your voice. It was an honor to sing with you one last time.

Also from YesYes Books

Full-length Collections

Heavy Petting by Gregory Sherl

Panic Attack, USA by Nate Slawson

I Don't Mind If You're Feeling Alone by Thomas Patrick Levy

The Youngest Butcher in Illinois by Robert Ostrom

If I Should Say I Have Hope by Lynn Melnick

Frequencies: A Chapbook and Music Anthology

Volume 1

Speaking American by Bob Hicok, *Lost July* by Molly Gaudry, and *Burn* by Phillip B. Williams plus downloadable music files from Sharon Van Etten, Here We Go Magic, and Outlands

Vinyl 45s

a print chapbook series

Please Don't Leave Me Scarlett Johansson by Thomas Patrick Levy

Pepper Girl by Jonterri Gadson

Poetry Shots

a digital chapbook series

Nocturne Trio
with poetry by Metta Sáma and art by Mihret Dawit

Toward What Is Awful
with poetry by Dana Guthrie Martin and art by Ghangbin Kim

How to Survive a Hotel Fire
with poetry by Angela Veronica Wong and art by Megan Laurel

The Blue Teratorn
with poetry by Dorothea Lasky and art by Kaori Mitsushima

My Hologram Chamber Is Surrounded by Miles of Snow
with poetry by Ben Mirov and images by Eric Amling